For My Sister

For My Sister

Reflections on Life, Love, and Sisterhood

Ariel Books

Andrews McMeel
Publishing

Kansas City

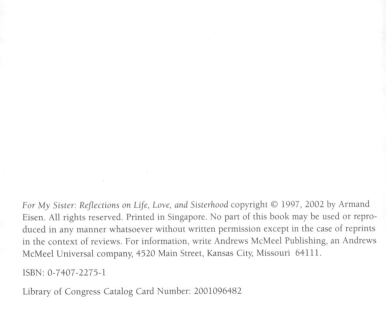

ISBN: 0-7407-2275-1

Library of Congress Catalog Card Number: 2001096482

Contents

Introduction

THEY SHARE OUR TOYS as children, borrow our sweaters (sometimes even remembering to ask) as teenagers, and, as adults, give us advice on love, money, and everything; *they* are our sisters. And whether we have one or several, we are blessed to be part of the wonderful and unique relationship that is sisterhood.

It is a relationship filled with love, rivalry, lots of memories, and, of course, friendship. Our friendship may have been strong from the very beginning or it may have evolved as we became adults; either way, we cherish our sisters. Having grown up with us, our sisters possess a unique understanding of who we are. Conversations with them are likely to be intimate and personal because we don't need to censor anything we say. This honesty can cause hurt feelings now and again, but our relationship is too deeply rooted, too strong to be felled by the occasional squabble.

The quotations that follow—on love, friendship, memories, childhood, family ties, and dreams—pay tribute to sisterly affinity. So read on and enjoy. 💔

Inseparable Companions

I could join with Diana and Mary in all their occupations; converse with them as much as they wished, and aid them when and where they would allow me. There was a reviving pleasure in this intercourse, of a kind now tasted by me for the first time—the pleasure arising from perfect congeniality of tastes, sentiments, and principles.

CHARLOTTE BRONTË
Jane Eyre

Your sister is your other self. She is your alter ego, your reflection, your foil, your shadow.

BARBARA MATHIAS

*O*h, the comfort, the inexpressible comfort of feeling safe with a person; having neither to weigh thoughts nor to measure words but to pour them all out, just as it is, chaff and grain together.

GEORGE ELIOT

In my friend,
I find a second
self.

ISABEL NORTON

$\mathcal{T}$here isn't much that I can do,

But I can sit an hour with you,

And I can share a joke with you,

And sometimes share reverses, too . . .

As on our way we go.

MAUDE V. PRESTON

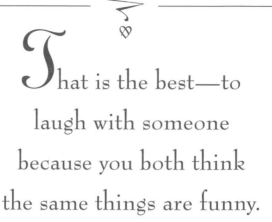

That is the best—to
laugh with someone
because you both think
the same things are funny.

GLORIA VANDERBILT

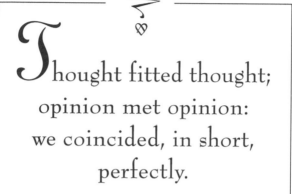

Thought fitted thought;
opinion met opinion:
we coincided, in short,
perfectly.

CHARLOTTE BRONTË
Jane Eyre

The difference between men friends and women friends is that men tend to do things together, women tend to just be together.

ART JAHNKE

The true test of friendship is to be able to sit or walk with a friend for an hour in perfect silence without wearying of one another's company.

DINAH MARIA
MULOCK CRAIK

*W*ho knows the joys of friendship.
The trust, security, and mutual
tenderness. The double joys where
each is glad for both.

NICHOLAS ROWE

[You] are different in detail of how you live your lives, but not in substance. Interchangeably, you go in and out of each other's shadows.

BARBARA MATHIAS

One recipe for friendship is the right
mixture of commonality and difference.
You've got to have enough in common
so that you understand each other and
enough difference so that there is
something to exchange.

ROBERT WEISS

*T*he attachment of the sisters was
exactly what Darcy had hoped to see.
They were able to love each other, even
as well as they intended. Georgiana had
the highest opinion in the world of
Elizabeth . . .

JANE AUSTEN
Pride and Prejudice

When two people love
each other they work
together always. . . . Joy is
shared; trouble is split.

Friendship is
one heart in
two bodies.

JOSEPH ZABARA

*F*riendship cheers like a sunbeam; charms like a good story; inspires like a great leader; binds like a golden chain; guides like a heavenly vision.

NEWELL D. HILLIS

Best friend, my
well-spring in
the wilderness!

GEORGE ELIOT

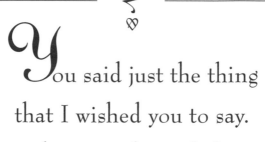

You said just the thing
that I wished you to say.
And you made me believe
that you meant it.

GRACE STRICKER DAWSON

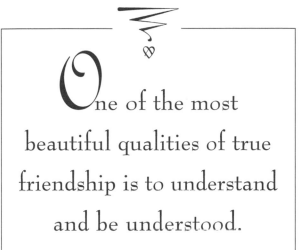

One of the most beautiful qualities of true friendship is to understand and be understood.

SENECA

*O*ur brothers and sisters are there with us from the dawn of our personal stories to the inevitable dusk.

SUSAN SCARF MERRELL

I liked to read what they liked to read: what they enjoyed, delighted me; what they approved, I reverenced.

CHARLOTTE BRONTË
Jane Eyre

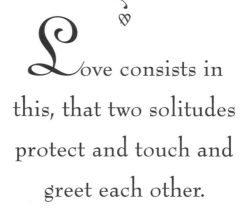

$\mathcal{L}$ove consists in
this, that two solitudes
protect and touch and
greet each other.

RAINER MARIA RILKE

*E*ver since Laura could remember, Carrie had been her little sister. First she had been a tiny baby, then she had been Baby Carrie, then she had been a clutcher and tagger, always asking "Why?" Now she was ten years old, old enough to be really a sister.

LAURA INGALLS WILDER
The Long Winter

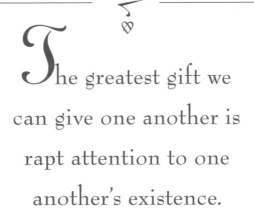

The greatest gift we can give one another is rapt attention to one another's existence.

SUE ATCHLEY EBAUGH

34

When we get to the rocking chair stage, we plan on living in very close proximity, either side by side or in the same house.

DIXIE CARTER
on her sister Midge

Familiarity
breeds content.

ANNA QUINDLEN

Hold a true
friend with both
your hands.

NIGERIAN PROVERB

To throw away an honest
friend is, as it were,
to throw your life away.

SOPHOCLES

Wherever I turn, in the house or out-
of-doors, I seem to see your face before my
eyes, and when I find myself deceived, and
realize that you are really gone, you will
understand how sore my distress has been—
nay, how great it still is.

BEATRICE D'ESTE

Ever the best of friends.

CHARLES DICKENS
Great Expectations

She slept three feet away. From across the ocean between us she described the glories she witnessed, the spectacle of a life worth living. She could look straight into the apartments across the street.

BONNIE FRIEDMAN

The ornament of
a house is the friends
who frequent it.

RALPH WALDO EMERSON

Reinforce the stitch
that ties us, and I will
do the same for you.

DORIS SCHWERIN

43

Woman is
woman's natural
ally.

EURIPIDES

We learn best to listen to our own voices if we are listening at the same time to other women . . . whose stories, for all our differences, turn out, if we listen well, to be our stories also.

BARBARA DEMING

$\mathcal{T}$he bond between
women is a circle—we
are together within it.

JUDY GRAHN

*F*riendship is a strong and habitual inclination in two persons to promote the good and happiness of one another.

EUSTACE BUDGELL

A friend is,
as it were, a
second self.

CICERO

I cannot deny that, now I am without your company I feel not only that I am deprived of a very dear sister, but that I have lost half of myself.

BEATRICE D'ESTE

Friendship,
one soul in
two bodies.

PYTHAGORAS

$\mathcal{F}$riendship . . . does not abolish distance between human beings but brings that distance to life.

WALTER BENJAMIN

Four sisters, parted for an hour,
None lost, one only gone before,
Made by love's immortal power,
Nearest and dearest evermore.
Oh, when these hidden stores of ours
Lie open to the Father's sight,
May they be rich in golden hours,
Deeds that show fairer for the light,
Lives whose brave music long shall ring,
Like a spirit-stirring strain,
Souls that shall gladly soar and sing
In the long sunshine after rain.

LOUISA MAY ALCOTT

Are we not like
the two volumes
of one book?

MARCELINE DESBORDES-
VALMORE

$\mathcal{F}$riendship is the only cement that will ever hold the world together.

WOODROW WILSON

*I*n thee my soul
shall own combined
The sister and the friend.

CATHERINE KILLIGREW

55

Encouragement and Support

For there is no friend like a sister
In calm or stormy weather;
To cheer one on the tedious way,
To fetch one if one goes astray,
To lift one if one totters down,
To strengthen whilst one stands.

CHRISTINA ROSSETTI

Two are better than one,
for if they fall, the one will
lift up his fellow.

ECCLES. 49:10

In the hour of distress and misery the eye of every mortal turns to friendship; in the hour of gladness and conviviality, what is our want? It is friendship.

WALTER SAVAGE LANDOR

Imps and angels simultaneously, they hover on the sidelines of all the other choices and connections—spouses, professions, children, friendships—that we make, sometimes lending a hand or ear but often simply taken for granted.

SUSAN SCARF MERRELL

$\mathcal{F}$riendship, a dear balm. . . .

A smile among dark frowns:

a beloved light:

A solitude, a refuge, a delight.

PERCY BYSSHE SHELLEY

*Y*et still my fate permits me this relief,

To write to lovely Delia all my grief.

To you alone I venture to complain;

From others hourly strive to hide my pain.

ABIGAIL COLMAN DENNIE

in a letter to her sister

The growth of true
friendship may be a
lifelong affair.

SARAH ORNE JEWETT

*I*n friendship unless, as we say, you see the naked heart and let your own be seen, there is nothing that you can deem trustworthy or reliable, not even the mere fact of loving and being loved, since you cannot know how genuine the sentiment is.

CICERO

$\mathcal{W}$oman softens her
own troubles by generously
solacing those of others.

FRANÇOISE D'AUBEGNE
MAINTENON

A faithful friend is a strong defense.

LOUISA MAY ALCOTT

$\mathcal{F}$riendship is always a
sweet responsibility, never
an opportunity.

KAHLIL GIBRAN

What do we live for,
if it is not to make life less
difficult for each other?

GEORGE ELIOT

When friends stop
being frank and useful to
each other, the whole world
loses some of its radiance.

ANATOLE BROYARD

*C*lare is really a people-person, which I'm not naturally, so she's taught me to relax, enjoy life, and not get so intense about everything.

CHRIS EVERT
on her sister

$\mathcal{A}$ woman, if she be really your friend, will have a sensitive regard for your character, honor, repute. She will seldom counsel you to do a shabby thing; for a woman friend always desires to be proud of you.

SIR EDWARD
BULWER-LYTTON

*I*t is the friends you
can call up at 4 A.M.
that matter.

MARLENE DIETRICH

$\mathcal{F}$riendship adds a brighter radiance to prosperity and lightens the burden of adversity by dividing and sharing it.

CARDINAL RICHELIEU

We all live on bases of shifting sands, [and] need trust.

ERMA J. FISK

*B*ecause of your firm faith, I kept the track
Whose sharp set stones my strength had almost
      spent—
I could not meet your eyes, if I turned back,
      So on I went.

Because of your strong love, I held my path
When battered, worn and bleeding in the
      fight—
How could I meet your true eyes, blazing wrath?
      So I kept right.

ANONYMOUS

Louise and Irlene always say
or do just the right things to
make me feel better.

BARBARA MANDRELL

. . . to my mother, who bought me my
first guitar, and to my sister, who is
my best critic, my best audience,
and my best friend.

TRACY CHAPMAN

Alone we can do so little; together we can do so much.

HELEN KELLER

*H*elp one another, is part of the religion of our sisterhood, Fan.

LOUISA MAY ALCOTT

Friendship is a sheltering tree.

SAMUEL TAYLOR
COLERIDGE

Two people holding each other up
like flying buttresses. Two people
depending on each other and babying
each other and defending each other
against the world outside.

ERICA JONG

*F*riendship needs no studied phrases,
   Polished face, or winning wiles;
Friendship deals no lavish praises,
   Friendship dons no surface smiles.

Friendship follows Nature's diction,
   Shuns the blandishments of Art,
Boldly severs truth from fiction,
   Speaks the language of the heart.

ANONYMOUS

81

The only thing to do is to
hug one's friends tight and
do one's job.

We need to take care of
ourselves, our relationships,
and reinforce our
connection to the world.

MELODY BEATTIE

$\mathcal{B}$ecause of their agelong training
in human relations—for that is what
feminine intuition really is—women
have a special contribution to make to
any group enterprise.

MARGARET MEAD

84

When do any of
us ever do
enough?

BARBARA JORDAN

$\mathcal{I}$f you have one true
Friend, you have more than
your share comes to.

THOMAS FULLER

It is not so much our
friends' help that helps us
as the confident knowledge
that they will help us.

87

When friendships are real, they are not glass threads or frost work, but the solidest things we can know.

RALPH WALDO EMERSON

$\mathcal{S}$ilences make the real
conversations between friends.
Not the saying but the never needing
to say is what counts.

MARGARET LEE RUNBECK

$\mathcal{A}$ true friend unbosoms freely, advises justly, assists readily, adventures boldly, takes all patiently, defends courageously and continues a friend unchangeably.

WILLIAM PENN

90

My friends are
my estate.

EMILY DICKINSON

There are three things that grow more precious with age; old wood to burn, old books to read, and old friends to enjoy.

HENRY FORD

I am not afraid to trust my sisters—not I.

ANGELINA GRIMKÉ

$\mathcal{I}$t seems to me that trying to live without friends is like milking a bear to get cream for your morning coffee. It is a whole lot of trouble, and then not worth much after you get it.

ZORA NEALE HURSTON

I felt it shelter
to speak to you.

EMILY DICKINSON

$\mathcal{A}$ friend is someone who understands your past, believes in your future, and accepts you today just the way you are.

SOLOMON

(P R O V E R B S 2 7 : 1 7)

There are good ships and there are bad ships, but the best ships are friendships.

CICERO

*I*t all starts with self-reflection.
Then you can know and empathize
more profoundly with someone else.

SHIRLEY MACLAINE

Each person grows not only by her
own talents and development of her
inner beliefs, but also by what she
receives from the persons around her.

IRIS HABERLI

Love from one being to another can only be that two solitudes come nearer, recognize and protect and comfort each other.

HAN SUYIN

(MRS. ELIZABETH COMBER)

$\mathcal{E}$ach contact with a human being

is so rare, so precious, one should

preserve it.

ANAÏS NIN

It is virtue, yes virtue, that initiates and preserves friendship. For it is virtue that is the source of the rational, the stable, the consistent element in life.

CICERO

$\mathcal{R}$espect . . . is appreciation of the *separateness* of the other person, of the ways in which he or she is unique.

ANNIE GOTTLIEB

A constant friend is a thing rare and hard to find.

PLUTARCH

The language of
friendship is not words
but meanings.

*I*f I can stop one heart from breaking,
I shall not live in vain;
If I can ease one life the aching,
Or cool one pain,
Or help one fainting robin
Unto his nest again,
I shall not live in vain.

EMILY DICKINSON

$\mathcal{A}$ friend is someone who
allows you distance but is
never far away.

NOAH BENSHEA

*E*ven though I can't solve your problems, I will be there as your sounding board whenever you need me.

SANDRA K. LAMBERSON

Female friendships that work are relationships in which women help each other to belong to themselves.

LOUISE BERNIKOW

What I expect from my male friends is that they are polite and clean. What I expect from my female friends is unconditional love, the ability to finish my sentences for me when I am sobbing, a complete and total willingness to pour their hearts out to me . . .

ANNA QUINDLEN

The time of discipline began.
Each of us the pupil of whichever
one of us could best teach what each
of us needed to learn.

MARIA ISABEL BARRENO

*A true friend
is the best
possession.*

BENJAMIN FRANKLIN

*Friendships
multiply joys,
and divide grief.*

THOMAS FULLER

argaret was silent. If her aunt could not see why she must go down, she was not going to tell her. She was not going to say: "I love my dear sister; I must be near her at this crisis of her life." The affections are more reticent than the passions, and their expression more subtle. If she herself should ever fall in love with a man, she, like Helen, would proclaim it from the house-tops, but as she only loved a sister she used the voiceless language of sympathy.

E. M. FORSTER
Howards End

The friendship that can
cease has never been real.

Love comforteth
like sunshine
after rain.

WILLIAM SHAKESPEARE
Venus and Adonis

$\mathcal{I}$ am a big believer that
you have to nourish
any relationship.

NANCY REAGAN

*Y*ou were there when I needed you. You stood above all of the others with your strength and you guided me. To each of you I offer my being, my love and all that I am.

DEIDRA SARAULT

$\mathcal{A}$ shadow in the parching sun,
and a shelter in a blustering storm,
are of all seasons the most welcome; so
a faithful friend in time of adversity,
is of all other most comfortable.

ANNE BRADSTREET

Gratitude is the
heart's memory.

FRENCH PROVERB

From quiet homes and first beginning,

Out to the undiscovered ends,

There's nothing worth the wear of winning,

But laughter and the love of friends.

HILAIRE BELLOC

We ought to be able to learn some things secondhand. There is not enough time for us to make all the mistakes ourselves.

HARRIET HALL

A faithful friend
is the medicine
of life.

ECCLES. 6:16

Without friendship and the openness and trust that go with it, skills are barren and knowledge may become an unguided missile.

JOHN D. ROCKEFELLER JR.

In love one has need of being believed; in friendship of being understood.

ABEL BONNARD

*I*ntimacies between women often
go backwards, beginning in revelations
and ending in small talk without loss
of esteem.

ELIZABETH BOWEN

There was a definite process by which one made people into friends, and it involved talking to them and listening to them for hours at a time.

REBECCA WEST

127

Sisters stand between
one and life's cruel
circumstances.

NANCY MITFORD

Character and Attitude

When fate knocks you flat on your back,
remember she leaves you looking up.

ANONYMOUS

$\mathcal{I}$'m going to turn on the light and
we will be two people in a room looking
at each other and wondering why on
earth we were afraid of the dark.

GALE WILHELM

*Y*ou've a deal more principle and
generosity and nobleness of character
than I ever gave you credit for, Amy.
You've behaved sweetly, and I respect
you with all my heart.

LOUISA MAY ALCOTT
Little Women

Now the foundation of that steadfastness and loyalty for which we are looking in friendship is trust, for nothing endures that cannot be trusted.

CICERO

We are all travellers in the wilderness of this world and the best that we find in our travels is an honest friend.

ROBERT LOUIS STEVENSON

We are here to add what
we can to, not to get what
we can from, life.

SIR WILLIAM OSLER

All the brothers were valiant, and all the sisters virtuous.

From the inscription on the tomb
of the Duchess of Newcastle
in Westminster Abbey

What matters most is
that we learn from living.

DORIS LESSING

*I*f there is any miracle in the world, any mystery, it is individuality.

LEO BAECK

One is taught by experience to put
a premium on those few people who can
appreciate you for what you are.

GAIL GODWIN

A friend is a
present you give
yourself.

ANONYMOUS

*C*aring about others, running the
risk of feeling, and leaving an impact
on people bring happiness.

RABBI HAROLD KUSHNER

How wonderful it is that
nobody need wait a single moment
before starting to improve the world.

ANNE FRANK

There is no outsider anywhere who wouldn't appreciate and even envy the tremendous advantage that sisters have, if properly utilized, against all odds.

SUSAN RIPPS

Happiness comes of the capacity
to feel deeply, to enjoy simply, to think
freely, to risk life, to be needed.

STORM JAMESON

*L*ife's under no

obligation to give us

what we expect.

MARGARET MITCHELL

*L*ife is easier than you'd think;
all that is necessary is to accept
the impossible, do without the
indispensable, and bear the intolerable.

KATHLEEN NORRIS

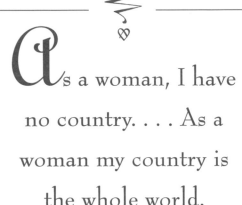

$\mathcal{A}$s a woman, I have no country. . . . As a woman my country is the whole world.

VIRGINIA WOOLF

The especial genius of women
I believe to be electrical in
movement, intuitive in function,
spiritual in tendency.

MARGARET FULLER

To believe a thing
impossible is to make it so.

FRENCH PROVERB

*I*n the long run the pessimist may
be proved right, but the optimist has
a better time on the trip.

ANONYMOUS

$\mathcal{T}$he door of success is marked
"push" and "pull." Achieving success
is knowing when to do what.

YIDDISH SAYING

Slowly we
adjust, but only
if we have to.

ELLEN GOODMAN

Sisters, whatever their stories, instinctively know how fortunate they are.

$\mathscr{I}$ recognize how crucial my relationship with my sisters is in the definition of my self.

BARBARA MATHIAS

Life is a negotiation.

WENDY WASSERSTEIN

$\mathcal{T}$he wise don't expect to find life worth living; they make it that way.

$\mathcal{T}$here ain't nothing
from the outside can
lick any of us.

MARGARET MITCHELL
Gone with the Wind

To live each day as though one's last, never flustered, never apathetic, never attitudinizing—here is the perfection of character.

MARCUS AURELIUS

$\mathcal{A}$lthough it may seem
That the process is slow,
Still, work is the yeast
That raises the dough.

MARY HAMLETT GOODMAN

Experience is what we
call the accumulation
of our mistakes.

$\mathcal{T}$here's a period of life when we swallow a knowledge of ourselves and it becomes either good or sour inside.

PEARL BAILEY

Let me listen
to me and not
to them.

GERTRUDE STEIN

No distance of place or lapse of time can lessen the friendship of those who are thoroughly persuaded of each other's worth.

ROBERT SOUTHEY

If we would build on a sure
foundation in friendship, we must
love our friends for their sakes
rather than for our own.

CHARLOTTE BRONTË

One pound of learning
requires ten pounds of
common sense to apply it.

PERSIAN PROVERB

$\mathcal{I}$t is not what we see and touch or
that which others do for us which makes
us happy; it is that which we think and
feel and do, first for the other fellow and
then for ourselves.

HELEN KELLER

*Y*ou gain strength, courage, and confidence by every experience in which you really stop to look fear in the face. You are able to say to yourself, "I lived through this horror, I can take the next thing that comes along." . . . You must do the thing you think you cannot do.

ELEANOR ROOSEVELT

Friendship without self-interest is one of the rare and beautiful things in life.

JAMES FRANCIS BYRNES

Confidence
begets
confidence.

LATIN PROVERB

When we can begin to take
our failures nonseriously, it means
we are ceasing to be afraid of them.
It is of immense importance to learn
to laugh at ourselves.

KATHERINE MANSFIELD

*H*appiness is not a
station to arrive at, but a
manner of traveling.

MARGARET LEE RUNBECK

*C*onfidence does more
to make conversation
than wit.

$\mathcal{L}$augh at yourself
first, before anyone
else can.

ELSA MAXWELL

Character, like embroidery, is made stitch by stitch.

Women have a way
of treating people more
softly. We treat souls
with kid gloves.

SHIRLEY CAESAR

There is a magnet in your heart that will attract true friends. That magnet is unselfishness, thinking of others first . . . when you learn to live for others, they will live for you.

PARAMAHANSA YOGANANDA

The quality of strength lined with tenderness is an unbeatable combination, as are intelligence and necessity when unblunted by formal education.

MAYA ANGELOU

A woman of honor should
not suspect another of things
she would not do herself.

MARGUERITE DE VALOIS

Sharing Our Dreams

Dreams are what you hope for, reality is what you plan for.

AMERICAN PROVERB

One is not born
a woman, one
becomes one.

SIMONE DE BEAUVOIR

$\mathcal{B}$elieving in our hearts that who
we are is enough is the key to a more
satisfying and balanced life.

ELLEN SUE STERN

$\mathcal{I}$'ve always believed
that one woman's success
can only help another
woman's success.

GLORIA VANDERBILT

*T*hey talk about a woman's sphere
  as though it had a limit;
There's not a place in earth or heaven,
There's not a task to mankind given,
There's not a blessing or a woe,
There's not a whispered "yes" or "no,"
There's not a life, or death, or birth,
That has a feather's weight of worth
Without a woman in it.

KATE FIELD

A woman is the full circle. Within her is the power to create, nurture, and transform.

DIANE MARIECHILD

Did you ever know that you're my hero?

LARRY HENLEY AND JEFF SILBAR
"Wind Beneath My Wings"

Just don't give up trying to do what you really want to do. . . . Where there's love and inspiration, I don't think you can go wrong.

ELLA FITZGERALD

$\mathcal{M}$ama exhorted her children at every opportunity to "jump at de sun." We might not land on the sun, but at least we would get off the ground.

ZORA NEALE HURSTON

Our way is not soft grass, it's a mountain path with lots of rocks. But it goes upwards, forward, toward the sun.

DR. RUTH WESTHEIMER

We older women who know we aren't heroines can offer our younger sisters, at the very least, an honest report of what we have learned and how we have grown.

ELIZABETH JANEWAY

We all live with the
objective of being happy;
our lives are all different
and yet the same.

ANNE FRANK

To be one woman, truly, wholly, is to be all women. Tend one garden and you will birth worlds.

KATE BRAVERMAN

Grasp what is good, even if it is meager; put your hand on it, hold onto it, and do not let it go.

BERECHIAH BEN NATRONAI

HA-NAKDAN

$\mathcal{I}$ didn't belong as a kid, and that always bothered me. If only I'd known that one day my differentness would be an asset, then my early life would have been much easier.

BETTE MIDLER

We can do no great
things; only small things
with great love.

MOTHER TERESA

$\mathcal{E}$verything in life is most fundamentally a gift. And you receive it best and you live it best by holding it with very open hands.

LEO O'DONOVAN

When you're young,
the silliest notions seem
the greatest achievements.

Each friend represents a world in us,
a world possibly not born until they
arrive, and it is only by this meeting
that a new world is born.

ANAÏS NIN

How many cares one loses
when one decides not to be
something but to be someone.

COCO CHANEL

Finish every day and be done with it. You have done what you could. Some blunders and absurdities no doubt crept in; forget them as soon as you can. Tomorrow is a new day; begin it well and serenely and with too high a spirit to be cumbered with your old nonsense. This day is all that is good and fair. It is too dear, with its hopes and invitations, to waste a moment on the yesterdays.

RALPH WALDO EMERSON

Far away there in the sunshine are
my highest aspirations. I may not reach
them but I can look up and see their
beauty, believe in them and try to
follow where they lead.

LOUISA MAY ALCOTT

From where you sit, you can probably reach out with comparative ease and touch a life of serenity and peace. You can wait for things to happen and not get too sad when they don't. That's fine for some but not for me. Serenity is pleasant, but it lacks the ecstacy of achievement.

ESTÉE LAUDER

200

We must not, in trying to think about how we can make a big difference, ignore the small daily differences we can make which, over time, add up to big differences that we often cannot foresee.

MARIAN WRIGHT EDELMAN

You can have anything you want if you want it desperately enough. You must want it with an inner exuberance that erupts through the skin and joins the energy that created the world.

SHEILAH GRAHAM

$\mathcal{N}$o good thing is
pleasant to possess,
without friends to share it.

SENECA

*I*t takes a lot of courage

to show your dreams

to someone else.

ERMA BOMBECK

There are two ways of
spreading light: to be
the candle or the mirror
that receives it.

EDITH WHARTON

I always wanted to be somebody.
If I made it, it's half because I
was game enough to take a lot of
punishment along the way and half
because there were a lot of people who
cared enough to help me.

ALTHEA GIBSON

I sought my soul,

But my soul I could not see.

I sought my God,

But my God eluded me.

I sought my sisters,

And I found all three.

ANONYMOUS

Family Memories, Family Ties

Do not save your loving speeches
For your friends till they are dead;
Do not write them on their tombstones,
Speak them rather now instead.

ANNA CUMMINS

I don't believe fine young ladies enjoy themselves a bit more than we do, in spite of our burnt hair, old gowns, one glove apiece, and tight slippers that sprain our ankles when we are silly enough to wear them.

LOUISA MAY ALCOTT
Little Women

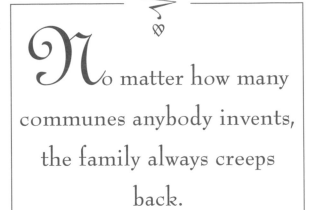

$\mathcal{N}$o matter how many communes anybody invents, the family always creeps back.

MARGARET MEAD

The family is
the nucleus of
civilization.

WILL AND ARIEL
DURANT

$\mathcal{L}$ove doesn't make
the world go 'round. Love
is what makes the ride
worthwhile.

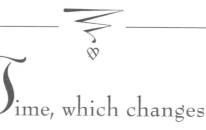

Time, which changes
people, does not alter
the image we have retained
of them.

MARCEL PROUST

*B*oth within the family and
without, our sisters hold up our mirrors:
our images of who we are and of who
we can dare to become.

E L I Z A B E T H   F I S H E L

I had a heritage, rich and nearer than the tongue which gave it voice. My mind resounded with the words and my blood raced to the rhythms.

MAYA ANGELOU

*O*ften, in old age, they become each other's chosen and most happy companions. In addition to their shared memories of childhood and of their relationship to each other's children, they share memories of the same home, the same homemaking style, and the same small prejudices about housekeeping that carry the echoes of their mother's voice.

MARGARET MEAD

One of the luckiest
things that can happen to
you in life is . . . to have
a happy childhood.

AGATHA CHRISTIE

Reproof a parent's province is;
A sister's discipline is this:
By studied kindness to effect
A little brother's young respect.

MARY LAMB

Women . . . often . . . need to return to their past, to the women who were part of that past, to girlhood when a self existed that was individual . . . almost as though with layers of roles and responsibilities they have covered over a real person and must now peel back those layers and reclaim the self that was just emerging in adolescence.

MARY HELEN WASHINGTON

When you're young and someone tells you what you are and shows you how to be proud, you've got a head start.

VIKKI CARR

I wanted to share the doll's house with Bridget . . . I knew that I loved Bridget very deeply and identified with her yearning as she tentatively touched the miniature grandfather's clock in the miniature hallway.

BROOKE HAYWARD
on her sister

When you look at your
life, the greatest happinesses
are family happinesses.

DR. JOYCE BROTHERS

A happy childhood
can't be cured. Mine'll
hang around my neck
like a rainbow . . .

HORTENSE CALISHER

What we remember from childhood we remember forever—permanent ghosts, stamped, imprinted, eternally seen.

CYNTHIA OZICK

The older I get the simpler my fantasies. Two women sitting across a table from each other, two cups of coffee, strong as the love.

PAM HOUSTON

$\mathcal{T}$he family [is] the
first essential cell of
human society.

POPE JOHN XXIII

Family jokes, though rightly cursed by strangers, are the bond that keeps most families alive.

What surprised me was that within a family, the voices of sisters as they're talking are virtually always the same.

ELIZABETH FISHEL

We can't give up our girls for a dozen fortunes. Rich or poor, we will keep together and be happy in one another.

LOUISA MAY ALCOTT
Little Women

One hears one's childhood and it is ancient.

KATHLEEN FRASER

To me, fair friend, you

never can be old

For as you were when first

your eye I eyed,

Such seems your beauty still.

WILLIAM SHAKESPEARE

Writing this, I realize how sweet and slippery is this word "sister"—big enough to stretch beyond biology and across time; flexible enough to define soulmates and virtual strangers; precise enough to embrace me and Rena, me and Betty, my two daughters, and all the sisterhoods in between.

LETTY COTTIN POGREBIN

Within our family there was no such thing as a person who did not matter. Second cousins thrice removed mattered. We knew—and thriftily made use of—everybody's middle name. We knew who was buried where. We all mattered, and the dead most of all.

SHIRLEY ABBOTT

$\mathfrak{M}$y sister! With that thrilling word
   Let thoughts unnumbered wildly spring!
What echoes in my heart are stirred,
   While thus I touch the trembling string.

MARGARET DAVIDSON

I will never forget the day after Martin's funeral, when you packed up your son and came to stay with me. The fact that I never had to ask meant so much to me. . . . I'm very lucky. I don't have a husband, but I do have a sister.

CORETTA SCOTT KING

If I had a sister, I would want
her to be older and knowledgeable,
flippant with her dark secrets. I
imagined a room full of underwear
and sophisticated underground music,
bras on the shower rod.

MONA SIMPSON

*A*s the standard bearers of our first families, our siblings are the only people who can truly share our happy and unhappy memories with us, who can help reconstruct that early sense that the world was manageable and we would always be cared for.

SUSAN SCARF MERRELL

*H*ome is not where you live but where they understand you.

CHRISTIAN MORGENSTERN

We wove a web

in childhood,

A web of sunny air.

CHARLOTTE BRONTË
Retrospection

Benevolence is the characteristic element of humanity, and the great exercise of it is in loving relatives.

TZE-SZE

*E*verywhere, we learn

only from those whom

we love.

GOETHE

A home-made friend
wears longer than one you
buy in the market.

AUSTIN O'MALLEY

She laid down her work and looked at her sister. She thought Gudrun so charming, so infinitely *charming*, in her softness and her fine, exquisite richness of texture and delicacy of line. There was a certain playfulness about her too, such a piquancy or ironic suggestion, such an untouched reserve. Ursula admired her with all her soul.

D. H. LAWRENCE
Women in Love

The human heart, at
whatever age, opens only
to the heart that opens
in return.

MARIA EDGEWORTH

244

It's a great
comfort to have
an artistic sister.

LOUISA MAY ALCOTT

*I*ntimate relationships cannot substitute for a life plan. But to have any meaning or viability at all, a life plan must include intimate relationships.

HARRIET LERNER

We are each other's reference point at our turning points.

ELIZABETH FISHEL

$\mathcal{B}$lessed be childhood, which
brings down something of heaven into
the midst of our rough earthliness.

HENRI FRÉDÉRIC AMIEL

Sons branch out, but one woman leads to another.

MARGARET ATWOOD

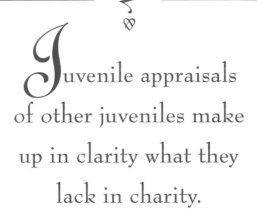

*J*uvenile appraisals
of other juveniles make
up in clarity what they
lack in charity.

EDGAR Z. FRIEDENBERG

You are a thing
of beauty and a
joy forever.

LOUISA MAY ALCOTT
Little Women

Childhood is the kingdom where nobody dies.

EDNA ST. VINCENT MILLAY

*B*rothers and sisters tend to be so completely different from each other that comparing oneself to a sibling is a little like Albert Einstein assessing his accomplishments in terms of Florence Nightingale's. Of course, one can draw such a comparison, but what purpose does it serve?

SUSAN SCARF MERRELL

*F*amily faces are magic mirrors.
Looking at people who belong to us, we
see the past, present, and future.

GAIL LUMET BUCKLEY

God gave us our
memories that we might
have roses in December.

SIR JAMES M. BARRIE

255

We thought we were running away from the grownups, and now we are the grownups.

MARGARET ATWOOD
Cat's Eye

Marcia was incredibly organized, obsessively neat. . . . I mean she folded her underwear like origami.

LINDA BARNES
"Lucky Penny"

The older I grow, the more
earnestly I feel that the few intense
joys of childhood are the best that
life has to give.

ELLEN GLASGOW

Call it a clan, call it a network, call it a tribe, call it a family. Whatever you call it, whomever you are, you need one.

JANE HOWARD

$\mathcal{Y}$es'm, old friends is
always best, 'less you can
catch a new one that's fit to
make an old one out of.

SARAH ORNE JEWETT
The Country of the Pointed Firs

$\mathcal{W}$e should not let

the grass grow on the

path of friendship.

MARIE-THÉRÈSE
RODET GEOFFRIN

What families have in common the world around is that they are the place where people learn who they are and how to be that way.

JEAN ILLSLEY CLARKE

$\mathcal{H}$eirlooms we don't
have in our family. But
stories we've got.

ROSE CHERNIN

There is always one moment
in childhood when the door opens
and lets the future in.

GRAHAM GREENE
The Power and the Glory

264

The desire to be and have a sister is a primitive and profound one that may have everything or nothing to do with the family a woman is born to. It is a desire to know and be known by someone who shares blood and body, history and dreams . . . [the] darkest secrets and the glassiest beads of truth.

ELIZABETH FISHEL

[*D*addy] said: "All children must look after their own upbringing." Parents can only give good advice or put them on the right paths.

ANNE FRANK

A ministering angel shall my sister be.

WILLIAM SHAKESPEARE
Hamlet

Our siblings. They resemble us just enough to make all their differences confusing, and no matter what we choose to make of this, we are cast in relation to them our whole lives long.

SUSAN SCARF MERRELL

An older sister helps
one remain half child,
half woman.

ANONYMOUS

After a certain age, the more one becomes oneself, the more obvious one's family traits appear.

*L*ove is the best
relationship, wisdom
the best ancestor.

JOSEPH ZABARA

Their errand was done and off their minds, and the sun was shining, the wind was blowing, the prairie spread far all around them. They felt free and independent and comfortable together.

LAURA INGALLS WILDER
The Long Winter

Our pattern of sisterhood makes an ongoing spiral, and within that spiral are our families, our communities, the earth, stars, all time. The spiral resembles two women carrying water through a battlefield in a rain of arrows. It resembles a long snake of relatives who walk through history, from the eastern hills of time immemorial. The light balances the dark. Wildness walks next to her steady sister. They make it to the other side together.

JOY HARJO

Other things may change
us, but we start and
end with the family.

ANTHONY BRANDT

Childhood smells
of perfume and
brownies.

DAVID LEAVITT

$\mathcal{T}$he happiest moments in
my life have been the few
which I have passed at home
in the bosom of my family.

THOMAS JEFFERSON

$\mathcal{L}$et us make one point . . . that
we meet each other with a smile,
when it is difficult to smile. . . . Smile
at each other, make time for each
other in your family.

MOTHER TERESA

To the family—that dear octopus from whose tentacles we never quite escape, nor, in our inmost hearts, ever quite wish to.

DODIE SMITH
Dear Octopus

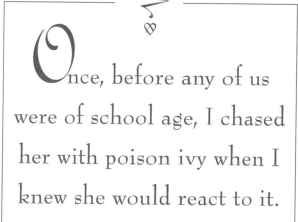

Once, before any of us were of school age, I chased her with poison ivy when I knew she would react to it.

JOY HARJO

We acquire friends
and we make enemies,
but our sisters come with
the territory.

EVELYN LOEB

I never tempted her with word
   too large:
But, as a brother to his sister, show'd
Bashful sincerity and comely love.

WILLIAM SHAKESPEARE
Much Ado About Nothing

I tell you of all history the most beautiful product is the family tie. Of it are born family consideration . . .

ZONA GALE
Miss Lulu Bett

You don't choose your family. They are God's gift to you, as you are to them.

ARCHBISHOP DESMOND TUTU

*L*ittle girls are the nicest things
that happen to people. They are born
with a little bit of angelshine about
them, and though it wears thin
sometimes there is always enough
left to lasso your heart.

ALAN BECK

One's family is
the most important
thing in life.

ROBERT C. BYRD

The apple
doesn't fall far
from the tree.

JEWISH PROVERB

*I*t may be of no moment to you; you have sisters, and don't care for a cousin; but I had nobody; and now three relations—or two, if you don't choose to be counted—are born into my world full grown. I say again, I am glad!

CHARLOTTE BRONTË
Jane Eyre

Sticks in a
bundle are
unbreakable.

KENYAN PROVERB

$\mathcal{I}$ have come back again to where I belong; not an enchanted place, but the walls are strong.

DOROTHY H. RATH

Sisterhood—that is, primary and bonding love from women—is, like motherhood, a capacity, not a destiny. It must be chosen, exercised by acts of will.

OLGA BROUMAS

The love that grew with us from our cradles never knew diminution from time or distance. Other ties were formed, but they did not supersede or weaken this. Death tore away all that was mortal and perishable, but this tie he could not sunder.

CHARLOTTE ELIZABETH
TONNA

Oft I see her when I sleep,

And her kiss feel on my brow;

But when morning comes, I weep,

Just as you do, Sister, now.

MARGUERITE BLESSINGTON

The inside of her was like the night sky on Independence Day, lit with the fireworks she loved, or the black-crayoned drawings she taught me to scratch with a pin, revealing rainbows of nighttime carnival underneath. She was the first person I met who had an actual internal life. How I wished I were she!

BONNIE FRIEDMAN

Old friends, like old wines, don't lose their flavor.

God borrows from many creatures to make a little girl. He uses the song of a bird, the squeal of a pig, the stubbornness of a mule, the antics of a monkey, the spryness of a grasshopper, the curiosity of a cat, the speed of a gazelle, the slyness of a fox, the softness of a kitten, and to top it all off He adds the mysterious mind of a woman.

ALAN BECK

The events of childhood
do not pass, but repeat
themselves like seasons
of the year.

ELEANOR FARJEON

To look at one's sister is to look
at the other and realize that even
with the most unflinching scrutiny,
all bets are off. To know a sister
is to know paradox.

PATRICIA FOSTER

Rivalry . . . and Reconciliation

Sometimes, sisters have the same journey in their hearts. One may help the other or betray her. Will they cross over? Will the ship sail without them?

LOUISE BERNIKOW

One can never speak
enough of the virtues,
the dangers, the power of
shared laughter.

FRANÇOISE SAGAN

299

$\mathcal{T}$he pull between sisters
is the realization of
similarity versus the need
for difference.

ELIZABETH FISHEL

300

Wishing to be friends
is quick work, but
friendship is a slow-
ripening fruit.

ARISTOTLE

301

She shared much with her sister. . . .
They had one bike and one sled
between them and had learned long ago
that these possessions were not worth
the fights.

ANN MCGOVERN

$\mathcal{L}$ittle girls are cute and small only to adults. To one another they are not cute. They are life-sized.

MARGARET ATWOOD

Sisters define their rivalry in terms of competition for the gold cup of parental love. It is never perceived as a cup which runneth over, rather a finite vessel from which the more one sister drinks, the less is left for the others.

ELIZABETH FISHEL

Jamie [Lee] and I have run the gamut from tearing each other's hair out when we were kids, to ignoring each other, to being each other's best friend.

KELLY CURTIS

$\mathcal{S}$isters is probably *the* most competitive relationship within the family, but once the sisters are grown, it becomes the strongest relationship.

MARGARET MEAD

I don't believe that the accident of birth makes people sisters or brothers. It makes them siblings. Gives them mutuality of parentage. Sisterhood and brotherhood is a condition people have to work at.

MAYA ANGELOU

$\mathcal{A}$ sister is both your
mirror—and your
opposite.

ELIZABETH FISHEL

What is exciting is not for one
person to be stronger than the other . . .
but for two people to have met their
match and yet they are equally as
stubborn, as obstinate, as passionate,
as crazy as the other.

BARBRA STREISAND

Family is just accident. . . .
They don't mean to get on your
nerves. They don't even mean to
be your family, they just are.

MARSHA NORMAN

$\mathcal{F}$ond as we are of our
loved ones, there comes at
times during their absence
an unexplained peace.

ANNE SHAW

*T*here is space within sisterhood
for likeness and difference, for the
subtle differences that challenge
and delight; there is space for
disappointment—and surprise.

CHRISTINE DOWNING

Comparison is a
death knell to
sibling harmony.

ELIZABETH FISHEL

*I*f we all discovered that we had only five minutes left to say all that we wanted to say, every telephone booth would be occupied by people calling other people to tell them that they loved them.

CHRISTOPHER MORLEY

$\mathcal{I}$ believe that basically people are people . . . but it is our differences which charm, delight, and frighten us.

AGNES NEWTON KEITH

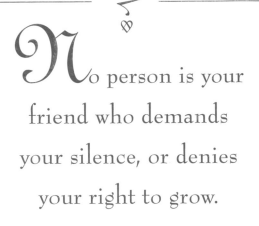

$\mathcal{N}$o person is your
friend who demands
your silence, or denies
your right to grow.

ALICE WALKER

When you fight with a brother or sister, you're only hurting yourself, because they are a part of you.

AMERICAN PROVERB

Competition is easier to accept if you realize it is not an act of oppression or abrasion. . . . I've worked with my best friends in direct competition.

DIANE SAWYER

Honest differences

are a healthy sign

of progress.

MOHANDAS (MAHATMA)
GANDHI

You can't give up a sister.
You were born with them
and you die with them.

ELIZABETH MEAD STEIG

$\mathcal{A}$ word of kindness
is better than a fat pie.

RUSSIAN PROVERB

$\mathcal{A}$ll living things evolve and are involved in a pattern of struggle and release. This includes sisterhood.

JOY HARJO

We share space in the family with them, we learn from them and teach them, we divide up parental loyalties with them, we envy them, admire them, dominate them, hate them, love them.

SUSAN SCARF MERRELL

What I
cannot love,
I overlook.

ANAÏS NIN

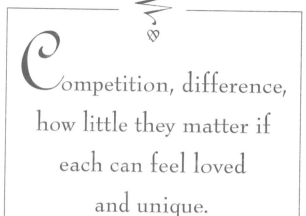

Competition, difference,
how little they matter if
each can feel loved
and unique.

ERIKA DUNCAN

325

$\mathcal{L}$ying in the cradle was my dearest friend and bitterest rival, my mirror and opposite, my confidante and betrayer, my student and teacher . . . my subordinate, my superior and, scariest still, my equal.

ELIZABETH FISHEL

$\mathcal{A}$nd what a delight
it is to make friends with
someone you have despised!

COLETTE

If you tell your sister to go to hell in twelve different languages and you need a quarter, you can say "I need a quarter" and she'll give it to you.

ELIZABETH MEAD STEIG

The richest love is that which submits to the arbitration of time.

LAWRENCE DURRELL

329

True friendship
is never serene.

MARIE DE SÉVIGNÉ

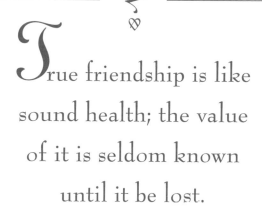

*T*rue friendship is like
sound health; the value
of it is seldom known
until it be lost.

CHARLES CALEB COLTON

Sibling rivalry is not
an evil born of parental
failure. It is a fact of life.

SEYMOUR V. REIT

As nobody can do more mischief to a woman than a woman, so perhaps might one reverse the maxim and say nobody can do more good.

ELIZABETH HOLLAND

*J*ust because we're sisters under
the skin doesn't mean we've got
much in common.

ANGELA CARTER

The problems that plague a friendship are rarely one hundred percent the other person's fault. We should self-examine carefully before we make up our mind—and before we close it.

JUDITH VIORST

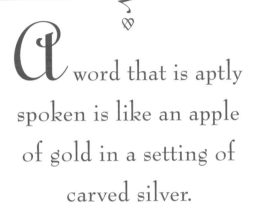

A word that is aptly spoken is like an apple of gold in a setting of carved silver.

Take away love
and our earth is
a tomb.

ROBERT BROWNING

I don't believe that one person heals another. I believe that what we do is invite the other person into a healing relationship. We heal together.

RACHEL NAOMI REMEN

The relationship between two siblings is perhaps more like a cactus than an oak, for it requires less watering than other friendships in order to survive.

SUSAN SCARF MERRELL

One drop of love
can create a sea
of tears.

JEWISH PROVERB

With patience, luck, and the will to change, the quarrels of the early years fertilize the soil in which friendship takes root.

ELIZABETH FISHEL

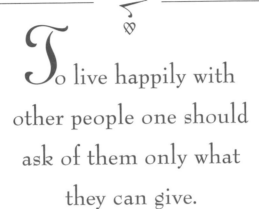

To live happily with other people one should ask of them only what they can give.

TRISTAN BERNARD

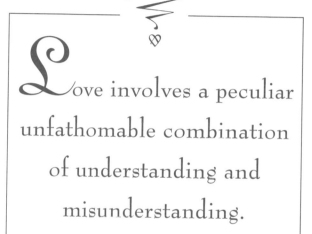

Love involves a peculiar unfathomable combination of understanding and misunderstanding.

DIANE ARBUS

$\mathcal{B}$ig sisters are the crab grass in the lawn of life.

CHARLES SCHULZ
Peanuts

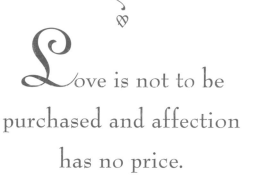

*L*ove is not to be
purchased and affection
has no price.

ST. JEROME

*A*nybody can be angry—that is easy; but to be angry with the right person, and to the right degree, and for the right purpose, and in the right way—that is not within everybody's power and is not easy.

ARISTOTLE

346

*F*rom the psychological jousting
between sisters in the early family arena
emerge the first tentative boundaries of
their personalities.

ELIZABETH FISHEL

Rivalry is better than envy.

MONGO PROVERB

$\mathcal{I}$ have come back full circle to my own sister, to the value of traversing an often troubling relationship, one that has fractured and sustained me, but most important, has helped me piece together the story of myself.

PATRICIA FOSTER

$\mathcal{H}$ow life catches up
with us and teaches us to
love and forgive each other.

JUDY COLLINS

Sometimes it's worse to win a fight than to lose.

BILLIE HOLIDAY

$\mathcal{A}$ sister can be seen as someone who is both ourselves and very much not ourselves—a special kind of double.

TONI MORRISON

The Power of Love

The story of a love is not important—what is important is that one is capable to love. It is perhaps the only glimpse we are permitted of eternity.

HELEN HAYES

$\mathcal{F}$riends are together when they are separated, they are rich when they are poor, strong when they are weak, and— a thing even harder to explain—they live on after they have died.

CICERO

Familiar acts
are beautiful
through love.

PERCY BYSSHE SHELLEY

$\mathcal{T}$he best and most beautiful things
in the world cannot be seen or
even touched. They must be felt
with the heart.

HELEN KELLER

[M]y sister is] a bowl of
golden water which brims
but never overflows.

VIRGINIA WOOLF

*Y*ou will find as you look back upon your life that the moments when you have really lived are the moments when you have done things in the spirit of love.

HENRY DRUMMOND

You think I love you from
complaisance and ask you to visit me
from politeness. I don't. I love you
because I love you.

LOUISE HONORINE
DE CHOISEUL

*T*he moment we exercise our affections,

the earth is metamorphosed: there is no

winter, and no night: all tragedies, all

ennuis vanish—all duties even.

RALPH WALDO EMERSON

The solidest friendship
is that of friends who
love one another.

EUDORA WELTY

*Love those
who love you.*

VOLTAIRE

An onion with
a friend is a
roast lamb.

EGYPTIAN PROVERB

Of all the means to insure happiness throughout the whole of life, by far the most important is the acquisition of friends.

EPICURUS

$\mathcal{L}$ove is an expression and assertion of self-esteem, a response to one's own values in the person of another.

AYN RAND

*I*n the arithmetic of love, one plus one equals everything, and two minus one equals nothing.

MIGNON MCLAUGHLIN

The love we give
away is the only
love we keep.

ELBERT HUBBARD

$\mathcal{T}$o love is to make

of one's heart a

swinging door.

HOWARD THURMAN

When somebody is
very dear,
A dream, anything,
nothing stirs your fear.

JEAN DE LA FONTAINE

To feel the love of people whom we love is a fire that feeds our life.

PABLO NERUDA

You meet your friend,
your face brightens—you
have struck gold.

KASSIA

There is only one
happiness in life, to love
and be loved.

GEORGE SAND

To love" means nothing but to cherish the person for whom one feels affection, without any special need and without any thought of advantage.

CICERO

This book was typeset in Bernhard
Modern and Linoscript by Nina Gaskin.

Book design by
Judith Stagnitto Abbate